# FEEL-GOOD GARDENING

FEEL-GOOD GARDENING

An Hachette UK Company
www.hachette.co.uk

Vie Books, an imprint of Summersdale Publishers Ltd
Part of Octopus Publishing Group Limited
Carmelite House
50 Victoria Embankment
LONDON
EC4Y 0DZ
UK

www.summersdale.com

Printed and bound in China

ISBN: 978-1-80007-991-5

Substantial discounts on bulk quantities of Summersdale books are available to corporations, professional associations and other organizations. For details contact general enquiries: telephone: +44 (0) 1243 771107 or email: enquiries@summersdale.com.

# FEEL-GOOD GARDENING

*How to Reap Nature's Benefits for Mental,
Physical and Spiritual Well-Being*

### CLAIRE STARES

# Contents

# INTRODUCTION

Many of us are on a quest for self-improvement. We want to increase our mental well-being, our physical state, our productivity and our connection with other people and the natural world. Well, did you know that gardening can make a dramatic difference in our ability to achieve all these goals? The World Health Organization defines good health as, "a state of complete physical, mental and social well-being and not merely the absence of disease or infirmity". Our sedentary, indoor, modern lifestyles can have a negative impact on our health and well-being, causing physical and mental illness.

American biologist and naturalist, Edward O. Wilson's biophilia hypothesis suggests that humans possess an innate urge to seek connections with other living things, but we find ourselves increasingly alienated from nature. Nature deficit disorder has been associated with higher rates of stress, anxiety,

chronic pain, obesity, diabetes, cardiovascular disease and many other conditions. For centuries, gardeners have known that their hobby can bring about a profound sense of calm and peace, strengthen and tone the body, inspire creativity and help to keep the mind sharp. Now, scientific research is emerging to support this intuitive understanding of the power of plants and the wider natural environment.

From revealing why growing plants can banish feelings of gloom and boost brain function to explaining how to maximize your garden workout, embrace the mindful aspect of gardening, or grow a community spirit, this book will give you the knowledge you need to realize your garden's full potential – as well as your own. It's also packed full of advice on garden design and creative ideas for garden projects and feel-good makes. So what are you waiting for...

**Dig in!**

# Part One: De-Stress While You Garden

Did you know that exposure to sunshine, plants and soil microbes can help you dig yourself out of depression? Or that listening to birdsong could boost your mental health? Connecting with nature through gardening can be a powerful antidote to the stresses and strains of modern life, boosting levels of happy hormones, helping you to find mental balance, reducing anxiety and encouraging you to relax and unwind.

Of all our senses, sight has the most immediate impact, but gardens are a feast for all the senses, offering a rich tapestry of sights, sounds, smells, textures and tastes which can help soothe and calm an overactive or troubled mind or invigorate and uplift the spirits. This chapter will teach you how to harness the power of nature to help you to de-stress and will provide you with top tips and creative ideas to turn your garden into a serene and restful sanctuary.

# CULTIVATE HAPPY HORMONES

The physical act of gardening increases the production of endorphins and dopamine – mood-boosting hormones which help to reduce stress, improve self-esteem, increase motivation, relieve pain and promote an overall sense of well-being. Gardening also significantly reduces levels of the stress hormone, cortisol. A continuously high level of cortisol in the body can increase the risk of mental health issues, headaches and sleep problems. It can also cause concentration and memory impairment, weight gain, reduced immunity, high blood pressure and heart disease. Just spending time in the garden can dramatically improve both your mental and physical health, and there are some simple ways to raise your levels of happy hormones:

- Plan a garden or border revamp or design a seasonal container display. Dopamine is triggered by the expectation of reward, so, by drawing up designs for your garden, you'll get a double hit of this mood-enhancing hormone, first during the planning and planting stage, and again when the flower buds, fruits or vegetables start to appear.

- Talk or sing to your plants. Scientists are still investigating whether communicating with our plants can make them grow bigger and stronger, but it's been proven that when we express love and care to them, we release feel-good neurochemicals, including endorphins, oxytocin and serotonin. So, go on, have a chat with your houseplants or serenade your flower beds!

# Fantastic Fractals

Nature is full of single geometric patterns that repeat thousands of times at different magnifications, from the forking branches of trees and leaf vein networks to the spiral whorls of pinecones, flower petals and even cauliflower florets. These patterns are known as fractals, and they have a unique soothing effect on the brain. Research has shown that looking at fractals can decrease stress and mental fatigue by up to 60 per cent and the calming effect is almost instantaneous. Fractals activate the parahippocampus, the region of the brain involved in emotion regulation and memory. They also increase alpha brainwave activity, enhancing the ability to focus and absorb new information, increasing creativity and boosting productivity. You don't even need to focus on the patterns; just being surrounded by them is enough to improve your mental health. If you can, try to spend at least 10 to 15 minutes in the garden every day and fill your home with fractal-rich houseplants.

Create a fractal-filled landscape by growing some of these plants in your garden:

- Sunflower (*Helianthus annuus*)
- Dahlia (*Dahlia* spp.)
- Rose (*Rosa* spp.)
- Boston fern (*Nephrolepis exaltata* "Bostoniensis")
- Mexican fleabane (*Erigeron karvinskianus*)
- Houseleek (*Sempervivum* spp.)
- Echeveria (*Echeveria* spp.)
- Globe artichoke (*Cynara cardunculus*)
- Romanesco cauliflower (*Brassica oleracea* var. *botrytis* "Romanesco")
- Sacred lotus (*Nelumbo nucifera*)
- Fennel (*Foeniculum vulgare*)
- Japanese maple (*Acer palmatum* spp.)

# THE BENEFITS OF BIRDSONG

There are few sounds more joyful than birds in full chorus, but birdsong is more than just pleasant background noise. Research shows that it can calm and comfort us during times of crisis and offers relief from stress and mental fatigue. It's believed that this healing effect may occur due to our evolution. For our ancestors, birdsong signalled safety, as birds don't sing when there are predators prowling nearby. Today, the trills and tweets are still a reassuring sound, promoting positivity. Another theory suggests that listening to birdsong gives the brain a break from cognitive challenges, helping us to relax and de-stress. There's no doubt that birdwatching encourages a mindful connection with nature and a recent study found that listening to birdsong can actually improve our mental well-being for up to eight hours. Scientists have also

found a correlation between happiness and the number of species present in residential areas. So, if you're keen to benefit from some bird therapy, tempt a greater diversity to visit your garden by providing them with a selection of feeders, locations to drink and bathe, and safe places to nest and roost. Then sit outside or throw open a window and enjoy the chorus of calming cooing calls and mood-boosting melodic songs.

Of the nearly 10,000 species of bird in the world, these are just some of the songsters you can seek:

- Blackbird
- Robin
- Blackcap
- Wood thrush
- House wren
- Northern mockingbird
- Northern cardinal
- Spotted dove

# MAKE A TEACUP BIRD FEEDER

Entice birds into your garden with a unique upcycled teacup and saucer bird feeder. Charity shops, thrift stores and flea markets are great places to find beautiful but inexpensive vintage china to use for this project.

## METHOD:

1. Wash the teacup and saucer and dry thoroughly.

2. Decide where to position the teacup on the saucer to ensure that it will hang nicely.

3. Squeeze a line of adhesive onto the outside of the cup, directly opposite the handle.

4. Positioning the teacup on its side with the handle pointing straight up, carefully press the cup onto the saucer. You may need to prop it in place while the adhesive dries.

5. Once the adhesive has set, thread a length of garden twine through the teacup's handle and secure it with a double knot. Tie another double knot at the other end of the twine to create a loop.

6. Hang your feeder from a branch and fill the cup and saucer with bird seed. If possible, position it so that you can watch the visiting birds through your window or from an outdoor seat.

# MY GARDEN BIRD LIST

Now that you've created a bird-friendly garden, find a relaxing spot to do some birdwatching and keep a record of the species that you see or hear (if you need some help with identification, download a birdsong app):

.................................................................................
.................................................................................
.................................................................................
.................................................................................
.................................................................................
.................................................................................
.................................................................................
.................................................................................
.................................................................................
.................................................................................
.................................................................................
.................................................................................
.................................................................................
.................................................................................

# TOP TIP

Keep bird tables, bird baths, feeders and the surrounding ground clean to prevent the spread of disease. Clear away bird droppings and mouldy food, as these can harbour harmful viruses, bacteria and fungi. Wash feeders regularly in hot, soapy water, rinse well and leave them to dry before refilling. Water containers should be scrubbed and rinsed out daily. Some diseases carried by wild birds can be transmitted to people or pets, so always use separate cleaning utensils, wear gloves, and wash your hands thoroughly once you've finished.

# Tree Therapy

**Shinrin-yoku** or forest bathing is a traditional Japanese relaxation practice. It's about being calm and quiet among trees, observing nature while breathing deeply. Recent research concluded that forest bathing can significantly reduce levels of the stress hormone cortisol, lower blood pressure and slow the heart rate. Also, trees secrete chemicals known as phytoncides, which boost our immune system function when breathed in. The good news is you don't need acres of woodland. Spending time beneath the leafy canopy of a single tree can be equally beneficial.

Here's how to treat yourself to some tree therapy:

- Turn off your mobile phone and fully immerse yourself in the sensory experience.

- Choose somewhere quiet to sit or lie down and engage in mindful observation. Notice small details – glimpses of birds flitting through branches, clouds scudding overhead or a beetle climbing the trunk. Breathe deeply. Consider how you feel.

- Listen to the sounds of birdsong, rustling leaves and creaking branches, or the soft patter of rain on leaves.

- Search for fractals in the branches and veins of leaves (see page 12 for more on the stress-busting power of fabulous fractals).

- Smell the tree resin, the damp earth, or the sweet scent of bluebells.

- If the mood takes you, stand up and hug the tree. Feel the strength of its trunk and the different textures of bark beneath your fingertips. Just like embracing another person, hugging a tree releases oxytocin, the cuddle hormone that makes us feel warm and fuzzy.

# TREEMENDOUS TREES

A Chinese proverb states: "The best time to plant a tree was 20 years ago. The second-best time is now." If you have space in your garden for at least one tree, and if you choose the right variety, you could be relaxing beneath its boughs in just a few years.

## HOW TO PLANT A TREE

1. Dig a hole the same depth, but three times as wide as the tree's root ball.
2. Loosen the root ball and stand the tree in a bucket of water to soak for at least half an hour if already moist and up to two hours if it is dry.
3. Place into the hole, so the top of the root ball is level with the surface of the soil.
4. Backfill the hole, making sure there are no air pockets around the roots. Firm the tree in, ensuring it's still standing straight.
5. Water well and add a layer of mulch.

Whether you have a balcony, compact courtyard garden, or sprawling acres, there's a tree for you. Here are six top contenders:

- **Acer** – Slow-growing and petite, with spectacular colour-changing foliage.
- **Magnolia** – Has magnificent goblet- or star-shaped flowers, which appear in early spring.
- **Birch** – Has tactile peeling silver bark and delicate light-filtering leaves.
- **Crab apple** – Compact, with beautiful spring blossom, followed by edible fruit.
- **Rowan** – Has frothy white blossom and vibrant edible berries beloved by birds.
- **Sweet gum** – Elegant, with attractive fissured bark and colourful autumn foliage.

# Shine On

Gardening provides the perfect opportunity to get outside and soak up some rays! Depending on where in the world you live, between 10–30 minutes of sun exposure on bare skin, several times a week, is recommended to ensure that you get enough vitamin D. A top tip to judge whether it's the optimal time of day to maximize vitamin D production is to look at your shadow – if it's the same height as you, or shorter, then your body will be able to manufacture vitamin D, but, if it's longer than you are tall, the sun isn't high enough in the sky to stimulate production.

Vitamin D is known as the "sunshine vitamin" for good reason. While small amounts can be absorbed from foods such as oily fish, red meat, egg yolks and mushrooms, exposure to direct sunlight is the most effective way for the body to produce it. A healthy dose has many benefits:

If you're going to spend a prolonged time outdoors, it's important to be sun safe by moving into the shade, applying sunscreen and covering up with suitable clothing.

- Increases the absorption of calcium and phosphate, which optimizes tooth and bone health, and reduces the risk of stress fractures and osteoporosis
- Supports muscle function

- Decreases the risk of heart disease
- Boosts immune function and the ability to fight diseases
- Helps to regulate mood and reduce the risk of depression

# Beat the Winter Blues

Gardening can also help to combat seasonal affective disorder (SAD), a type of depression that is often more severe during autumn and winter. SAD affects people in different ways, but common symptoms include depression, lethargy, irritability, sleep problems, overeating and feeling unsociable. Wrapping up warm and venturing outside to plant bare-root trees and shrubs, rake leaves, or tidy up containers, will maximize your exposure to sunlight, but even indoor gardening can be beneficial if you're tending plants positioned on a windowsill or next to patio doors. The physical activity of gardening releases endorphins, which can alleviate SAD symptoms.

# FEEL-GOOD FACT

Did you know that a single teaspoon of soil can contain up to one billion bacteria? Some of these microorganisms do more than just nourish plants. Scientists have discovered that the "friendly" soil microbe, Mycobacterium vaccae, has anti-inflammatory and immune-regulating properties and can stimulate the production of the neurotransmitter serotonin, which increases happiness and reduces anxiety and depression. It's believed that these mood-boosting bacteria may be inhaled when the soil is disturbed by digging, absorbed through the skin, or ingested in trace amounts when we eat homegrown fruit and vegetables – an excellent reason to get your hands dirty!

# Keep Calm and Garden On

Gardening offers many opportunities to engage in activities which can redirect our mental focus away from anxiety-inducing stimuli and negative thoughts. Rhythmic, repetitive motions have a meditative effect, calming the brain. Tasks like mowing the lawn, raking leaves, digging, seed-sowing and weeding can soothe the sympathetic nervous system, which is responsible for triggering the body's fight-or-flight response and, when overactive, can cause anxiety, panic attacks and insomnia. Gardening has also been shown to increase alpha waves, the brainwaves associated with rest and relaxation, and reduce beta waves, the brainwaves which mainly occur when we are mentally alert and focused.

# Relaxing Garden Retreats

There's no better place to de-stress than a garden retreat – a secluded nook in which to drink your morning coffee, meditate, read a book or simply sit back and enjoy the fruits of your labour – quite literally if you have an apple tree or blackberry bush! Unwind under the boughs of a tree, beneath a fragrant rose-covered arbour or inside a living willow den. Even if your garden retreat is simply a corner of your balcony or terrace, you could furnish it with a tree stump stool, a comfy outdoor beanbag or, for ultimate relaxation, a hammock.

# BUILD A SWEET PEA TEPEE

This living tepee will become a beautiful and fragrant retreat throughout the hot summer months and has the added bonus of providing food for pollinating insects and bunches of intensely perfumed cut flowers for brightening up your house.

## YOU'LL NEED:

10 thick 2 m (7 ft) – 3 m (10 ft) long bamboo canes or hazel bean poles

Garden twine

Chicken wire

A packet of sweet pea seeds or 20 sweet pea plants

If you'd prefer a retreat that is both beautiful and productive, substitute the sweet peas with climbing runner beans or French beans.

## METHOD:

1. Choose a level, sunny location with well-drained but moisture-retentive soil.

2. Push the canes or poles securely into the ground to form a circle large enough to sit inside.

3. Space them evenly, leaving a gap for the entrance.

4. Gather the canes or poles together crossing them over around 20 cm (8 in.) from the top to create a tepee shape and secure them with twine.

5. Wrap the structure with chicken wire, securing it with twine.

6. Sow two seeds or plants at the base of each cane or pole and water in.

7. Protect the seedlings from slugs using a non-toxic barrier (see page 88).

8. As the plants grow, encourage them to climb the chicken wire, gently tying them in with twine. Water regularly. Once the sweet pea flower buds begin to appear, start feeding every two weeks with a high potash fertilizer, e.g. tomato or comfrey feed.

9. Frequently picking the blooms will encourage the plants to keep flowering for as long as possible.

# STIMULATE YOUR SENSES

For many people, the garden is a place to escape the stresses of everyday life and forget their worries. If you're keen to create a space that will encourage you to relax and unwind or boost your mood, considering the senses is an excellent place to start. Incorporating a mixture of soothing and energizing sights, sounds, textures, tastes and scents will offer maximum "soft fascination", which occurs when your attention is held but your brain doesn't have to work too hard, allowing your mind to wander and providing the opportunity for reflection, introspection and recovery from mental fatigue.

- **Sight** – Consider colour, visual texture, shape and movement. Create layers of interest by planting larger, architectural plants at the back of displays and smaller, more delicate plants at the front.

- **Sound** – Think about growing flowers to attract songbirds and buzzing bees, and plants that will

create soft swishing sounds when the wind blows through their foliage. Introduce water features and windchimes to enhance natural noises and create a calming atmosphere.

- **Touch** – Include lots of tactile plants. The fuzzy, felty foliage of lamb's ear or silver sage are irresistible to stroke, while you'll want to run your fingers through witchgrass's decorative plumes.

- **Taste** – There are so many delectable plants to grow, from mouth-watering alpine strawberries to crisp cucumbers and pungent herbs to spicy edible flowers like nasturtiums and calendulas. Be adventurous!

- **Smell** – It's impossible to pass a lavender bush or scented-leaf geranium without crushing the foliage to inhale the floral aromas, so place sweet-smelling plants towards the front of your borders and use them to line paths.

# Choose Soft, Tranquil Tones and Rainbow Hues

A garden colour scheme based on soothing shades of green, white, blue and lavender is the easiest way to create a calm oasis, bringing balance and inviting inner peace. A vibrant palette of red, orange, yellow and pink can uplift your mood, encouraging feelings of happiness, energy and optimism. When planning your floral displays, make sure there will be year-round colour. A garden in winter is characterized by muted neutrals – brown, beige and grey – which can negatively impact our emotions. However, an injection of fiery-stemmed dogwoods, cheery pansies or bold cyclamens will brighten even the darkest of days.

# Glorious Green

As well as being nature's dominant colour, green is also very restful for the human eye, making it a top choice for relaxation. An abundance of verdant foliage will transform your garden into a calm sanctuary. To maximize the impact, layer plants with contrasting appearances, leaf shapes, textures and patterns. Plants like ferns, hostas, ivy and sweet woodruff create a woodland atmosphere, while bamboos, bananas, cannas and gingers give a tropical jungle vibe. A green palette can also include flowers such as:

- Aquilegia "Lime Sorbet"
- Bells of Ireland
- Chrysanthemum "Froggy"
- Clematis "Green Passion"
- Hellebore "Green Marble"
- Hydrangea "Limelight"
- Tulip "Spring Green"
- Zinnia "Envy"

# MAKE YOUR GARDEN SCENT-SATIONAL

The importance of scent is often underestimated. However, many fragrances have the power to alter our mood to create feelings of tranquillity, alleviate stress, ease insomnia or provide clarity and focus. When it comes to designing an aromatherapy garden, the first step is to consider location. Use highly perfumed flowers, aromatic herbs and plants with fragrant foliage to surround outdoor seating, dining or meditation areas. You can also grow them in window boxes, so their fragrance will gently waft inside your home. You can't go wrong with sweet-scented favourites like roses, sweet peas, lilac, jasmine, honeysuckle, lavender and scented narcissi. For heady night-time scent, grow evening primroses, night-scented stocks, night phlox, nicotiana, moonflower and angel's trumpets.

# LAVENDER DREAM PILLOW

Slip a lavender-filled pillow inside your pillowcase to help you drift off.

## YOU'LL NEED:

2 squares of fabric measuring 14 cm (5½ in.) x 14 cm (5½ in.)
Needle and thread
Dried lavender
Kapok stuffing
Ribbon

## METHOD:

1. Place the squares together, right sides facing in and sew around three sides, leaving a 2-cm (⁴/₅-in.) border.

2. Turn the pillow inside out and fill with a mixture of dried lavender and stuffing.

3. Fold over the top of the pillow and sew shut.

4. Wrap the ribbon around the pillow and tie it in a bow.

# Part Two: Improve Your Cognitive Health While You Garden

Gardening isn't just beneficial for physical health. Tasks like digging, raking and weeding boost your heart rate and oxygenation levels, which, in turn, increases blood flow to the brain. Tending a garden requires planning, researching and problem-solving and these activities create new neural pathways, enhancing learning and memory. A garden is also a canvas for creative expression. Research shows that being creative and learning new skills can help protect against memory loss and dementia as well as increasing confidence, self-esteem and life satisfaction. Whatever your level of experience, you can learn much from your garden, including the importance of patience, persistence and mental resilience. Plants themselves play a vital role in maintaining optimal brain health and enhancing cognition. Just being in their presence can significantly increase psychological well-being but they also improve indoor and outdoor air quality and provide us with nutrient-rich, brain-nourishing fruits and vegetables.

# GROW YOUR KNOWLEDGE

Every day's a school day in the garden! Whether you're a novice or a green-fingered expert, there are always opportunities to learn and develop. Research on brain health tells us that adults who keep their brains active by engaging in intellectually stimulating activities may help lower their risk of developing cognitive impairment or dementia. Problem-solving and learning new skills can also improve cognitive performance, reduce closed-mindedness and build confidence. So why not:

- Learn the Latin names of plants. With some plants having several different common names, getting to know scientific names can avoid confusion.

- Learn to identify the birds, mammals, amphibians, reptiles and insects that visit your garden.

- Grow new species of plants and learn what conditions and care they require.

- Learn a new skill, like seed-saving, aquascaping or topiary.

- Attend a workshop. Whether you're keen to learn how to prune fruit trees, grow vegetables or photograph plants, there's a class for you. Check out your local college or see what's available online.

- Study for a professional horticultural qualification. From practical horticulture to garden design, colleges and universities offer an array of fascinating courses, many of which can be studied part-time. Who knows – you might embark on a new career!

# TOP TIP

All plants have two main Latin names written in italics, the genus and the species, e.g. *Rosa gallica*. The genus represents a group of plants with a common ancestor, which share similar characteristics, while the species relates to a sub-group of one or more plants within the genus. Many botanical names offer clues about the plant's traits, such as the appearance of the leaves or flowers, preferred growing conditions or place of origin. For example, the scientific name for the sweet pea is *Lathyrus odoratus*, with lathyrus being a genus of flowering plants in the legume (pea and bean) family and odoratus meaning fragrant.

# Embrace Novelty

It's easy to get stuck in a rut but variety is the spice of life so try to avoid over-reliance on gardening routines. Doing something new, whether that be growing a certain type of plant for the first time, tasting an unusual vegetable, embarking upon a garden project or learning a new horticultural technique, will stimulate your imagination and creativity, exciting your brain and helping it to grow stronger and more resilient. Novelty is so important to human well-being that scientists have identified "neophilia", the desire to have novel experiences, as a predictor of longevity and happiness.

# DESIGN YOUR DREAM GARDEN

Planning is a fundamental cognitive skill that will help you to make the most of your space whether you're planting up a windowsill terrarium or have acres of land to play with. It's likely that your garden plans will evolve over years or even decades. However, the practice of setting goals is scientifically proven to keep you focused on and moving towards your target; it does this by changing the structure of your brain so that it's optimized to learn and adapt – a phenomenon known as neuroplasticity.

One of the best ways to visualize how you would like your garden to look, and the elements you'd like to incorporate, is to create a vision board. You can do this digitally on Pinterest or make a physical collage by attaching drawings, photos and magazine tear-outs to a large corkboard or sheet of cardboard.

Designing a garden is a deeply personal process so take time to brainstorm your ideas and look for inspiration:

- **In books and magazines (look at fashion, interiors and nature titles in addition to those dedicated to horticulture)**
- **In seed catalogues**
- **On Instagram, YouTube and Pinterest**
- **By visiting gardens (as well as visiting well-known tourist attractions, look out for open garden events)**
- **By attending exhibitions, fairs and horticultural shows**

# Go with the Flow

Do you ever pop outside intending to spend 15 minutes weeding and find yourself still pottering in the garden hours later, having lost all sense of time? You were "in the zone", or what psychologists refer to as "flow" – a state of mind that occurs when you're fully immersed in an activity. Achieving a flow state can help you feel greater enjoyment, making the task at hand more rewarding and fulfilling. As flow often occurs when you're doing something that you're good at, learning new garden skills and seeking new creative challenges will help you attain it.

# Grow Your Resilience

Pest invasions, diseases and crop failures can happen to all gardeners but your plants are resilient and so are you!

Top tips for increased resilience:

- **Adapt** – Don't give up; consider how to address the problem and take action.

- **Learn from experience** – Reflect on strategies that have helped you through past difficulties.

- **Remain hopeful** – While you can't change the past, you can draw on your inner strength and maintain an optimistic outlook.

- **Reach out** – Ask other gardeners for advice and support.

# Unleash Your Inner Artist

Art therapy is a relatively new practice but research has found that creating art can:

- Reduce stress and lower cortisol levels.
- Improve focus and help you achieve a flow state.
- Improve self-awareness and help you process emotions.
- Improve communication skills and foster self-expression.
- Help you make decisions.

Any type of creative expression allows you to engage with your environment. However, creating art inspired by plants you've grown or made using natural materials you've gathered will deepen your connection with your garden.

# TRY BLIND CONTOUR DRAWING

Blind contour drawing can help you to hone your observation skills and capture the essence of plants. It can also be a very meditative, calming exercise.

Choose your subject. Look closely at it, examining every detail. Put your pen or pencil to your paper and begin to draw, keeping your gaze fixed on the plant. Your eyes and pen or pencil should be moving in sync. Don't look down at your drawing! Start by drawing the outline, then work inwards, and finally add shading. The more details you notice, the more details you will draw on the page.

# CREATE A GARDEN MASTERPIECE

Opportunities for creativity are abundant in the garden, as there are so many natural materials you can use to create paintings, collages or ephemeral sculptures. Here are just a few ideas:

- Make natural inks and use them to paint a picture or make leaf prints. Fill a small jar with crushed flower petals or leaves and cover them with boiling water, then leave overnight to steep. In the morning, add a pinch of salt and ¼ teaspoon of vinegar to fix the colour, then strain the liquid through a fine mesh sieve into a clean jar. Alternatively, mash berries through a sieve to extract their pigments, then mix with a splash of water.

- Create an ice sculpture. Arrange flowers, foliage, berries and other natural items in containers of water (any freezer-safe container will do). Leave the containers outside overnight to freeze, or if the outdoor temperature isn't cold enough, put them in your freezer until they are solid. Carefully knock the ice shapes out of the containers and hang them from a tree or stack them into a sculpture, using a little water as glue to stick them together.

- Create a picture or 3D sculpture using leaves, petals, twigs, berries, seed heads and pinecones. Design a mandala pattern, create a fiery spiral of autumn leaves in shades of red, orange and gold, capture a beautiful sunset scene or make a portrait of a visiting bird.

# BRAIN-BOOSTING HERBS

Rosemary (*Rosmarinus officinalis*) has long been referred to as the herb of remembrance, but recent research has confirmed that this aromatic Mediterranean plant can significantly enhance cognition, boost memory and improve speed and accuracy when undertaking mental tasks. Simply pick a stem and crush the needle-like leaves between your fingers to inhale the pungent camphor scent or steep it in hot water and inhale the vapour.

The botanical name for sage (*Salvia officinalis*) is derived from the Latin "salvus", which means to save or heal and explains the herb's historical use as a brain-enhancing tonic. Several studies have shown that sage has potent antioxidant and cognition-enhancing properties, so add a handful of leaves to soup or roast them with vegetables.

Scientists have also discovered that drinking peppermint tea can improve alertness, while inhaling the aroma has been proven to enhance memory. Peppermint (*Mentha x piperita*) is one of the easiest herbs to grow in the garden or on a windowsill, and there is an array of delicious varieties to choose from including chocolate, lemon and black peppermint.

## FRESH MINT TEA

To make the perfect cup of flavourful mint tea, harvest a generous
handful of leaves and give them a
light scrunch to release the aromatic
oils. Drop the leaves into a teapot,
pour in boiling water, and leave to
infuse for 5 minutes until the liquid
turns golden green. Strain into a cup
and serve hot or chill in the fridge
and serve over ice for a refreshing
cold drink.

# BUILD A HERB SPIRAL

Beautiful and functional, herb spirals are space-saving raised beds constructed in the shape of a snail shell. They are tallest in the centre and spiral down to ground level, so offer different growing conditions within a single bed. This clever design means that they can accommodate a range of herbs. Mediterranean herbs like basil, rosemary, sage, thyme and oregano will thrive in the sunny and well-drained centre while shade-tolerant chives, parsley and coriander can be grown at lower levels. As mint can be thirsty and invasive, it's best planted near the base where it has room to sprawl and the soil is more moist.

Locate your herb spiral close to the house so you can easily pop outside to snip a few sprigs. Ideally, the site should be flat and receive full sun for at least part of the day. You can build the structure from bricks, stones, pavers, logs, or even empty upturned wine bottles. First, mark out your design. You can make your spiral as large as you'd like, but between 1–2 metres (3⅓–7 feet) in diameter is ideal. Dig a shallow

trench around the perimeter to secure your first layer of building materials, then build the walls from the outside in, increasing the height as you approach the centre. Once the walls are complete, put a thin layer of gravel in the base for drainage, fill the spiral with peat-free, multi-purpose compost and plant your herbs, watering them in well.

# BRAIN FOOD

We are what we eat! So why not have a go at growing your own brain-nourishing superfoods – plants which offer maximum nutritional benefits and are rich in compounds considered beneficial for cognitive health.

Dark red and purple berries including blueberries, blackberries, blackcurrants and aronia berries contain anthocyanins – protective compounds which may improve or delay short-term memory loss. If you only have a small space, look out for compact container or hanging basket varieties.

Tomatoes contain lycopene, a powerful antioxidant which may help to protect against the free radical cell damage that occurs during the development of dementia. Purple-skinned varieties also contain high levels of anthocyanins. Grow your tomatoes in direct sun to ensure they will fully ripen.

Pumpkin seeds contain zinc, an important trace mineral for normal brain function and enhanced memory. Miniature "Munchkin" varieties are ornamental climbing plants and the seeds can be roasted and eaten whole.

Leafy green vegetables including kale, spinach, collard greens and broccoli contain high levels of vitamin K, which is linked to improved memory and enhanced cognitive function, and vitamin C, which is believed to increase mental agility and reduce the risk of age-related brain degeneration. Pigeons and caterpillars are partial to the leaves, so protect plants with horticultural fleece or old net curtains.

Walnuts contain vitamin E, which studies suggest is vital for the prevention of cognitive decline, due to its powerful antioxidant action. Walnut trees should be planted in a sheltered location to prevent strong winds or spring frosts from damaging the blossom and reducing nut production.

# Pollution-Busting Plants

Urban air pollution continues to rise at an alarming rate and exposure to even low levels is associated with poor cognitive performance and age-related mental decline. Happily, plants can help protect you against pollution. Hedges make excellent air pollution barriers, particularly if your garden backs onto a road. Look out for super-plant cotoneaster (*Cotoneaster franchetii*) which scientists have discovered is 20 per cent more effective at capturing toxic airborne particles than other shrubs due to its hairy leaves. If you don't have room for a hedge, a green "living" wall will improve air quality and enhance any space, from an urban courtyard garden to the side of your house or shed. Here are three simple projects:

- Attach trellis or vine eyes and wire, then train climbers such as honeysuckle, jasmine, clematis, rambling or climbing roses, or pyracantha over the framework.

- Paint lengths of gutter pipe and attach them to a wall or fence, using brackets. Add compost, ensuring you block the ends of the pipes to prevent spillage. Pipe planters are perfect for growing shallow-rooted plants like sempervivums or cut-and-come-again salad leaves.

- Paint or stain a repurposed wooden pallet, fix it to a wall, then either wedge appropriately sized plant pots into the gaps between the slats or create planting pockets by lining the gaps with an old compost bag with holes poked into it for drainage and securing with staples. Fill with herbs, alpine strawberries, dwarf tomatoes or ferns.

# CREATE AN INDOOR JUNGLE CONTAINER

This tropical rainforest-inspired container will create an attractive, stress-relieving and brain-boosting indoor display, while the lush foliage will help to purify the air, removing carbon dioxide and the airborne pollutants emitted by synthetic carpets, soft furnishings, paints and detergents.

## YOU'LL NEED:

A large, watertight container

Horticultural grit

Houseplant compost

A selection of houseplants, e.g. peace lily (*Spathiphyllum wallisii*), spider plant (*Chlorophytum comosum*), blue star fern (*Phlebodium aureum*), bird's nest fern (*Asplenium nidus*), parlour palm (*Chamaedorea elegans*), raindrop peperomia (*Peperomia polybotrya*), and mosaic plant (*Fittonia albivenis*).

## METHOD:

1. Pour a 10-cm (4-in.) layer of grit into the base of the container.
2. Fill with compost until two-thirds full.
3. Remove the plants from their pots and arrange them in the container.
4. Pour in more compost to fill in the gaps and firm the plants in.
5. Water, then top the compost with a layer of grit.
6. Water whenever the compost feels dry.

# Plants for a Quiet Life

From traffic and aircraft to construction work and loud music, noise pollution impacts millions of people, causing stress, sleep disturbance and impaired attention. Noise isn't just annoying; according to the World Health Organization, it's a dangerous environmental threat to our health. Planting thick, bushy shrubs like holly, juniper, hawthorn or photinia is one of the most effective ways to dampen noise seeping into your garden, while a row of leafy houseplants positioned on the windowsill will help to sound-proof your home – the bigger the plant, the more sound it can naturally absorb.

# Natural Distractions

Some background noises, like the drone of distant traffic or the hum of electrical equipment, are irritating rather than dangerous. Here's how you can harness the power of the elements to mask them:

- **Install a water feature** – A solar-powered fountain floating in a wildlife pond or reflecting pool creates a continuous, soothing sound of trickling water. Rain chains attached to guttering or hung in trees emit musical tones every time there's a downpour.

- **Grow plants that "sing" when a breeze blows through them** – Grasses like golden oats and Amur silver grass rustle and whisper, while sweetcorn foliage swishes, mature bamboo stems make a melodic knocking noise and the seed pods of love-in-the-mist rattle softly.

# Garden Gratitude

The act of expressing gratitude builds emotional awareness and is associated with numerous well-being benefits, including improved motivation, mood and sleep quality. While it's understandable to feel downhearted if slugs munch their way through your vegetable plot or a favourite houseplant shrivels up and dies, focus on the positives instead with a weekly gardening gratitude journal. Think about your garden and gardening experiences. What are you thankful for? What has made you feel joyful? Who has helped you on your gardening journey? Be as specific as possible and jot down your reflections. The chances are that you'll soon see your garden in a more favourable light.

# GIVING THANKS

Nurturing plants and spending time outdoors in nature reminds us of the miracle of life, the beauty surrounding us and the people and wildlife that enrich our gardening experience. Use this space to record your gratitude.

Today I'm grateful for...

.............................................................

.............................................................

.............................................................

.............................................................

.............................................................

.............................................................

.............................................................

.............................................................

.............................................................

.............................................................

.............................................................

.............................................................

.............................................................

# Part Three: Get Fit While You Garden

Gardening is an undeniably enjoyable and relaxing pastime, but is it exercise? Yes! Research shows that regular gardening has the same health benefits as playing sport or attending an exercise class, improving your physical health, toning your body, releasing feel-good endorphins and helping you sleep better. While joining a gym may be convenient, you can't watch wildlife, smell the flowers, snack on freshly picked berries or appreciate the ever-changing natural landscape and weather when you're pounding away on a treadmill. Doesn't it make perfect sense to combine your daily exercise with your passion for gardening? The joy and satisfaction of seeing flowers bloom or harvesting fruit will motivate you to undertake physical activity more frequently and there's evidence to suggest that exercise can actually feel easier when performed in a natural environment. This chapter will help you to get the most out of your garden gym.

# A Prescription for Gardening

Gardening is good for you! It's a fact most gardeners already know – you feel and see the benefits every time you step outside. But now these benefits are being acknowledged by medical professionals, who are increasingly adopting green social prescribing. This involves referring patients to community gardening and food growing projects to boost their physical and mental health.

Gardening health benefits include:

- Preventing and managing diseases such as diabetes, cardiovascular diseases and cancer.
- Lowering blood pressure.
- Increasing cardiorespiratory fitness.
- Improving muscle and bone health and function.
- Improving balance and reducing the risk of falls and fractures.
- Helping to maintain a healthy body weight.

# A HEALTHIER HARVEST

You can double up on the health benefits of gardening by growing fruit and vegetables to fuel and nourish your body. As well as tasting delicious, your homegrown harvest is likely to be higher in essential vitamins and minerals than shop-bought produce. As you can pop outside and pick what you need when you need it, it will be at peak ripeness and freshness when it reaches your plate. According to one study, most produce loses 30 per cent of its nutrients within three days of harvesting, while spinach can lose up to 90 per cent of its vitamin C after just 24 hours.

# FEEL THE BURN

The World Health Organization recommends that adults aged between 18 and 64 should do at least 150 to 300 minutes of moderate-intensity aerobic physical activity or 75 to 150 minutes of vigorous-intensity aerobic activity a week to improve overall health and well-being. Globally, one in four adults fails to meet these recommendations. An hour of moderate-intensity gardening burns around 250 to 300 calories – comparable to half an hour of jogging, cycling or swimming. Planting, harvesting, weeding and watering are perfect warm-up activities, while high-intensity aerobic activities like digging, mowing the lawn and turning compost will get your heart pumping. The number of calories you'll burn is dependent on several factors including your weight, age, fitness level and the intensity at which you work. You can amp up your garden workout by switching power tools and electric lawnmowers for manual versions.

Average calories burned per 30 minutes:

- Watering – 60
- Cleaning tools – 120
- Harvesting fruit and vegetables – 125
- Weeding – 150
- Planting out seedlings – 160
- Raking leaves – 160
- Mulching – 175
- Lawn mowing – 175
- Pruning shrubs and cutting hedges with manual tools – 200
- Digging and shovelling – 250

# STRETCH AND TONE

Gardening is a full-body workout that will stretch and tone all your muscles, including some you probably didn't know you had! Using a hand trowel or fork to cultivate a container will target your triceps and biceps, while trimming hedges with hand shears will work the pectoral muscles in your chest. The squeezing action of secateurs will help to increase flexibility in your hands. If you're keen to tone your hamstrings, calves and glutes, use a spade or fork to plant a tree or double dig a vegetable bed. The actions of raking and hoeing are excellent for strengthening the upper and lower back, shoulders, chest and arms, while pushing a loaded wheelbarrow engages all the major muscle groups, including the abs.

If you'd like to take your workout to the next level, incorporate some of these exercises:

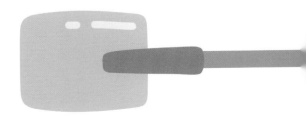

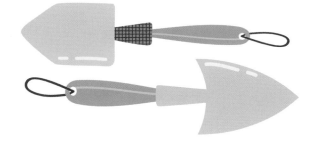

- Before you start mowing the lawn, hold onto the handle of the mower with both hands and do some heel raises, lifting onto your tiptoes, then slowly lowering your feet back down.

- Before you start digging, stick your spade vertically into the ground, then hold onto the handle and do some squats.

- Do some standing push-ups against a mature tree or the side of a shed.

- Release your shoulders and back muscles by holding a garden rake or broom horizontally across the back of your shoulders. Keeping your hips facing forwards, gently move your shoulders to one side and then the other, twisting from the waist.

# WATER WEIGHTLIFTING

Weight training isn't just about bulking up and building muscle mass. Lifting weights burns calories, increases strength, boosts metabolism, improves muscle tone and definition and can help correct posture and improve mobility. But forget the dumbbells. All you need is a couple of watering cans! Fill them up and do some farmer's walk exercises up and down the garden. This workout has the added benefit of giving your plants a good soak. Aim to train three times a week. It's important to incorporate rest days and allow your body to repair itself between sessions. This schedule is also perfect for most garden plants, which benefit from less frequent but more thorough watering to reach their deep roots.

### FARMER'S WALK EXERCISE:

- Place the full watering cans on the ground, one next to each foot.

- Squat down and grab a can in each hand.

- Engaging your core, pull your shoulder blades down and back as you carefully stand upright, lifting the cans.

- Step forward and begin walking up and down the garden. Keep your head up, shoulders back and core muscles engaged.

- Do some reps! You can perform this exercise for a set time or distance.

# SPICE UP YOUR LIFE

Growing your own spices isn't just a great way to pep up your meals. Ginger and chillies make attractive houseplants and have a host of health benefits.

**Ginger** – calms the digestive system and wards off nausea. It contains gingerol, a potent anti-inflammatory compound that can help reduce the pain of arthritis, exercise-induced inflammation and muscle soreness. Studies also suggest it may support heart health, lower high blood pressure and help manage cholesterol.

Plant rhizomes in a seed tray with the eyes facing upwards and cover with a few centimetres (1 in.) of multi-purpose compost. Once the roots and shoots appear, transplant into pots of compost, covering the rhizomes, but leaving the stems uncovered. Position in a warm, partially shaded location. Keep well-

watered but allow the pots to drain. Harvest in late summer when the plants stop producing leaves.

**Chillies** – contain capsaicin. The heat this compound produces can increase your metabolic rate, causing your body to burn more calories. Capsaicin also helps lower cholesterol and reduce the risk of suffering a blood clot, stroke or heart attack. Chillies are also rich in vitamins which help support the immune system.

Sow chillies from seed or buy plants from the supermarket or garden centre. Pot them up in a free-draining, peat-free, multi-purpose compost. Prevent the plants from getting leggy and ensure the chillies fully ripen by growing them on a warm, sunny, south-facing windowsill. Water little and often. Once flowers start to appear, feed weekly with liquid tomato feed.

# TAKE YOUR WORKOUT OUTSIDE

If you already have a regular exercise routine that you enjoy, why not swap the gym or your living room for something leafier and try an alfresco workout? Whether you're skipping, hula hooping or sweating through a HITT (High Intensity Interval Training) workout, exercising in the garden can add another level of challenge, as the undulating terrain will make your body work harder to maintain balance and stability. Plan your space. For some activities, you'll need room to run or jump, while for yoga or Pilates, you'll want a sheltered place to lay your mat, perhaps beneath a flower-covered pergola.

# Join an Outdoor Gym

If you don't have any outdoor space of your own, why not consider joining a nature conservation or community group that runs free outdoor gym sessions? These fun, free, social outdoor sessions focus on improving volunteers' health and fitness while transforming local nature reserves and green spaces. You will be guided in undertaking practical conservation activities such as growing food, tree planting, sowing wildflower meadows or establishing wildlife ponds, and there are jobs for every level of ability, fitness and experience.

# Yoga for Gardeners

Yoga increases flexibility, strength, balance and muscle building, making it an excellent activity for gardeners. If you take your yoga mat outside, you'll benefit from a daily dose of vitamin D and the ability to connect meaningfully with nature. Give this series of stretches a go:

**Mountain pose** – Try this pose any time you need to ground yourself and connect with the earth. Stand tall with your feet parallel and 10–15 cm (4–6 in.) apart, weight evenly balanced, and arms by your sides with your palms facing forwards. Spread your toes and press your feet into the ground.

**Tree pose** - From mountain pose, bend one knee and place your foot on the inside thigh of your opposite leg. Your knee should be pointing out to the side. Keep pressing your foot and thigh against each other and engage your core muscles, symbolically rooting yourself to the ground. Bring your hands into prayer position or raise your arms up to the sky. Hold the pose for 30–60 seconds. Gazing at a fixed point will help you to keep your balance.

**Wide-legged forward fold** – This pose encourages stability when you're pruning or weeding. Stand with your legs wide apart and feet parallel. Root your feet into the ground through the toes, pads and heels. Engage your abdominal muscles, lengthen your spine, and bend forwards from the hips, bringing your hands to the ground. Keep your back straight and knees soft.

**Butterfly pose** – Digging can strain your lower back, hips and inner thighs. This pose will prevent your muscles from stiffening up. Begin in a seated position. Gently bend your knees and press the soles of your feet together. Sit up straight, draw your shoulders down and back. Interlace your fingers around your toes or place your hands on your shins or ankles, positioning your feet closer to your hips.

**Child's pose** – Gardeners often find themselves on their hands and knees when weeding and planting. This pose provides respite for tired legs by gently stretching the knees, thighs and hips. Spread your knees as wide as your mat. Let your belly rest between your thighs, with your bottom touching your heels. Rest your forehead on the floor and stretch your arms out in front of you with your palms on the ground.

# HERBAL MAT SPRAY

If you're taking your yoga mat out into the garden, it's bound to get a bit grubby. This easy-to-make natural disinfectant spray smells divine and will keep things clean and fresh.

## METHOD:

1. Pour the witch hazel into the jar. Add the herbs and lemon peel, completely submerging them.

2. Infuse for three weeks, shaking daily.

3. Use the funnel to pour the witch hazel into the spray bottle.

4. Add the water.

5. Shake well before use. Spritz over your mat and allow it to sit for 2–3 minutes, then wipe with a cloth and leave to air dry.

**YOU'LL NEED:**

60 ml (2 fl oz) witch hazel
Jam jar
Sprigs of fresh herbs
Lemon peel
Muslin-lined funnel
150-ml (5-fl oz)
   spray bottle
60 ml (2 fl oz) water

# FEEL-GOOD FACT

The key to keeping healthy starts with protecting your
DNA. Telomeres are protein caps found at the tips of
chromosomes, which protect our genes from damage. They
shorten as we age, affecting our health and lifespan. But
studies show that endurance exercise like gardening increases
the production of the enzyme telomerase, which has the
ability to increase the length of telomeres and slow down the
ageing process, keeping us fit and active for longer.

# Grow Your Five a Day

Evidence suggests that eating at least three portions of vegetables and two portions of fruit every day is associated with a reduced risk of developing many diseases, including cancer, heart disease, stroke and respiratory diseases. If you have a fruit and vegetable patch in the back garden, it's easy to pick a handful of blueberries to top your breakfast porridge, harvest fresh salad leaves and cherry tomatoes for lunch, and serve your homegrown kale, squash, courgettes, beetroot or beans for dinner, with a dish of strawberries for dessert. Growing your own also allows you to experiment with hard-to-buy produce, like Jerusalem artichokes, oca, kohlrabi and aronia berries.

# PLAN A FRUIT AND VEG PATCH

Whether you have a garden, allotment, balcony or window box, you can grow your own.

- Concentrate on cultivating fruits and vegetables you love eating along with those that are expensive to buy in the supermarket like herbs, salad leaves and berries. Produce that tastes better eaten fresh from the plant, such as tomatoes, is also a great bet. If you have limited time or space, avoid crops that take up a lot of room or have a long growing season, such as cabbages and parsnips.

- Consider how many plants you need. Courgettes are super productive with a single plant producing up to four fruit a week, whereas you'll need to keep sowing cut-and-come-again lettuce leaves every two weeks if you want salad throughout the summer.

- All you need to sow seeds is a good peat-free seed compost and a container. Repurposed plastic food tubs or egg cartons make excellent seed trays. Peas and beans like a long root run; you can make root trainer pots from cardboard toilet paper tubes.

- Square foot gardening is a clever growing method that maximizes the use of space in a raised bed or border. Simply divide your space into a grid of 30 cm (1 ft) squares and sow or plant different kinds of vegetables in one or more squares. The size of the plants at maturity determines the number you can fit in each square. For example, you could sow 16 radishes or eight dwarf peas but only one tomato plant.

# Go Organic

If you choose to garden organically, your homegrown fruit and vegetables are guaranteed to be free from harmful pesticides, reducing your chemical burden. According to the World Health Organization, pesticide residues in food are potentially toxic to humans and may be associated with allergies, reproductive health problems, autoimmune diseases and an increased risk of certain types of cancer. Organic produce can be expensive to buy in the shops so it's more cost-effective to grow your own.

Unfortunately, pests and diseases are an inevitable part of gardening, but there are many ways to protect your crop against damage without resorting to harmful chemicals. Here are some top tips:

**Slugs and snails** – Use human hair, coffee grounds, eggshells or straw pellets to create a physical barrier around plants. If you're growing in containers, try sticking copper tape around the circumference, as this gives pests a mild shock. Make a slug trap by leaving empty grapefruit shells upside down on the soil overnight. The slugs will gather inside and can be disposed of the next morning. Encourage hedgehogs, frogs, toads and newts into your garden as they will happily munch on pesky molluscs.

**Aphids, whiteflies, blackflies, thrips, mealybugs and scale insects** – Make a natural insect spray by blitzing one bulb of garlic, two chillies and a litre (34 fl oz) of water in a blender. Leave it to stand for 10 minutes, then strain to remove the solids. Decant into a spray bottle and spray liberally on affected plants. Plant pollen-rich flowers to encourage ladybirds and lacewings, as the adults and their larvae can consume 50–100 aphids a day.

**Fungal diseases** – Powdery mildew affects many plants, including courgettes, cucumbers, squash and peas. The main cause is lack of water, particularly if this is followed by waterlogging. On a warm, dry morning, mix one part milk with nine parts water and lightly spray onto the affected leaves. Repeat after a fortnight.

**Butterfly and moth caterpillars** – Plant sacrificial food plants, e.g. a patch of nettles, and net your brassicas to prevent the adults from laying their eggs.

**Birds** – Net brassicas or cover them with horticultural fleece. Grow berries inside a fruit cage or cut up old tights to make protective sleeves to slip over fruit-laden branches.

**Deer** – The most effective way to deter hungry deer is to keep them out of the garden using robust fencing. Tree guards will help protect young fruit trees. Human hair stuffed into a muslin bag and hung in bushes at head height is also said to keep them away.

**Invasive weeds** – Smother with a thick layer of cardboard weighed down with bricks. Alternatively, carefully pour over boiling water or use white vinegar which will kill the weed but is child, pet and wildlife safe.

**Rabbits and squirrels** – Use physical barriers such as fencing or wire cloches to deter nibbling. They may also avoid the smell of garlic, onions and peppermint.

**Sawfly larvae** – Plant poached egg plant (*Limnanthes douglasii*) to attract hoverflies, which are their natural predators.

# PREVENT ACHES AND PAINS

While gardening can offer a great workout, it's important to protect yourself against injury. Here's how:

- Before you start gardening, warm up your muscles with stretches and a brisk walk around your plot.

- Stay hydrated by drinking plenty of water (pep it up with fresh mint from the garden).

- Pace yourself. Don't tackle all your gardening jobs at once and take regular breaks.

- Switch tasks regularly to prevent repetitive activities like digging, raking and weeding from causing muscle strain.

- Change hands when carrying a heavy watering can back and forth.

- Lift with your legs not your back. Crouch rather than bend, engage your core muscles and keep the weight close to your body as you lift.

- Don't tackle heavy-lifting tasks alone. If you need to move a large plant, container or bag of compost, use a wheelbarrow or ask someone for a helping hand.

- Use a foam knee pad to reduce pressure on your joints.

- If you struggle to bend, invest in long-handled or telescopic tools and consider installing raised beds or plant pot stands.

- If your muscles are aching, have a soak in a herb-infused Epsom salt bath and then rub a soothing muscle balm over the affected areas.

- Listen to your body. Pain is a warning sign that you need to stop what you're doing and rest. If pain persists, seek medical advice.

# SORE MUSCLES HERBAL BATH SOAK

If you've overdone it in the garden, use anti-inflammatory, pain-relieving herbs to make this fragrant, muscle-relaxing bath soak.

## YOU'LL NEED:

200 g (7 oz) Epsom salts
100 g (3½ oz) bicarbonate of soda (baking soda)
   A mixing bowl
200 g (7 oz) fresh herbs or 100 g (3½ oz) dried herbs, e.g.
   calendula, chamomile, clary sage, ginger root, hibiscus,
   juniper berries, lavender, lemon verbena, meadowsweet,
   peppermint, rose petals, rosemary, thyme
A large muslin fabric bag or a long cotton sock
A length of string or ribbon

## METHOD:

1. Mix the Epsom salts and bicarbonate of soda together in a bowl.

2. Gather your herbs and roughly chop any long or woody stems, then add them to the bowl and stir well.

3. Pour the salt and herb mixture into a muslin bag or sock and tie the top securely.

4. Drop the bag or sock into a warm running bath or hang it from the tap, so the water runs through it. Give it a good squeeze to get out every drop of herb-infused water.

If you're using fresh herbs, you'll need to use your bath soak on the day you make it. A batch made with dried herbs can be stored in an airtight jar for up to six months.

# Part Four: Find Spirituality While You Garden

Spirituality is the concept of a belief in something beyond the self and the recognition that there is more to being human than our physical and sensory experiences. Being fully present and tuning into your surroundings can enable you to cultivate a more harmonious relationship with your garden and also

recognize that you are part of nature.
Watching a seed germinate and grow
encourages us to contemplate creation
and the miracle of life and to experience
a child-like sense of awe and wonder.
Recognizing that there is something
greater than yourself can help you to
cope with life's challenges and provide a
sense of comfort. Whether you believe in
a higher power or seek meaning through
your connection to the natural world, the
exercises in this chapter will encourage
you to slow down and find peace and a
sense of purpose.

# You've Got to Have Faith

Gardening is a profound act of faith. We sow seeds in the belief that the dormant embryos will awaken and seedlings will burst into life. We plant and tend gardens trusting that they will grow and flourish, providing a bounty of beautiful, life-enhancing flowers and delicious, life-sustaining fruit and vegetables. Gardening connects us to the changing seasons, reminding us that everything is transitory. We may face decline and decay in autumn and winter but spring and summer herald rebirth, renewal and the emergence of new life. So, in the words of Audrey Hepburn, "To plant a garden is to believe in tomorrow."

# FEEL-GOOD FACT

The texts of many world religions make reference to gardens, which typically represent heaven or paradise on Earth. They serve to remind us that humans bear responsibility for the world created by the divine and that we have a duty to treat nature with care and respect, preserving it for generations to come. Religion has also inspired the creation of many sacred gardens, often attached to places of worship. These spiritual sanctuaries offer respite and encourage quiet reflection, meditation and prayer.

# Garden Meditation

Meditation has a host of benefits, from relieving anxiety and depression to improving concentration and attention. If your thoughts are cloudy or you're experiencing a creative block, stepping outside and meditating can focus your mind and reset your thinking. The garden is the perfect place to practise meditation away from household distractions. All that's required is a comfortable, quiet place to sit.

- Begin your meditation with an intention. State it clearly out loud: "I will listen to the sounds of the birds and insects." "I will feel the warmth of the sun on my skin." "I will appreciate every breath of fresh air."

- Close your eyes and focus on your breathing. Notice the sensation of the fresh air entering your nostrils and filling and leaving your lungs as you inhale through your nose and exhale through your mouth. Breathe regularly, letting each breath flow deep into your stomach.

- Do a body scan. Working from head to toe, pay attention to the sensations in your body. If you've been gardening, do you notice any tension, aching muscles or sore spots, or do you feel energized?
- Now tune in to the sounds of the garden. Listen to the breeze rustling the leaves, birds singing, insects buzzing, water trickling, or perhaps silence. If your mind starts to wander, acknowledge the thought without judgement, let it go, and gently return your awareness to your breath and the natural soundtrack.
- Aim to meditate for 10 to 15 minutes a day, so it becomes an established daily routine.

# GROW YOUR OWN MEDITATION SEAT

If you plan to meditate in the garden regularly, having a dedicated spot to sit will provide consistency and help to focus your energy. This rustic living seat will help you to connect physically to the earth, and when you sit on the cushion of fragrant herbs, they will release their aroma, promoting relaxation and helping you to focus your mind and build a spiritual connection with your garden.

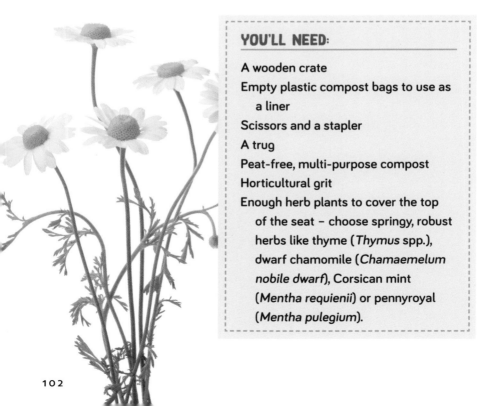

## YOU'LL NEED:

A wooden crate

Empty plastic compost bags to use as a liner

Scissors and a stapler

A trug

Peat-free, multi-purpose compost

Horticultural grit

Enough herb plants to cover the top of the seat – choose springy, robust herbs like thyme (*Thymus* spp.), dwarf chamomile (*Chamaemelum nobile dwarf*), Corsican mint (*Mentha requienii*) or pennyroyal (*Mentha pulegium*).

## METHOD:

1. Cut the compost bags to fit the inside of your wooden crate and snip some holes at the base for drainage.

2. Staple the bags in place to create your liner.

3. In the trug, mix two-thirds compost with one-third horticultural grit.

4. Fill the crate or box with the compost mix, leaving 2–3 cm (⁴/₅–1 in.) of space between the surface of the compost and the edge of the container.

5. Carefully remove the herbs from their pots and gently tease out the roots.

6. Plant them evenly, so they will spread out and cover the surface.

7. Firm the herbs in and water them well.

8. Give them a month or so to root strongly before you start sitting on them.

9. Check the compost moisture levels regularly, watering the plants if it feels dry.

# Garden Affirmations

Affirmations are powerful and positive statements that aim to support, motivate or challenge you in some way, tapping into both your conscious and unconscious mind. Repeating affirmations during meditation can be a great way to affirm the way you want to live your life, manifest self-confidence, focus on positives and uplift your mood. Pick one of these examples, or better still, create your own:

- My garden is nurturing me and helping me flourish.

- I am at one with nature and nature is at one with me.

- I will grow strong like my plants.

# My Garden Affirmations

Affirmations hold more significance and power when you write them yourself. They should be optimistic expressions so include words like "I will", "I am" and "I have". Use this page to create a list of personal affirmations:

..............................................................................
..............................................................................
..............................................................................
..............................................................................
..............................................................................
..............................................................................
..............................................................................
..............................................................................
..............................................................................
..............................................................................
..............................................................................

# ROSE PETAL MEDITATION BEADS

Meditation beads take on special significance if crafted from flowers that you've grown. Touching each bead as you repeat an affirmation can help focus the mind and encourages breath control.

## YOU'LL NEED:

Petals from approximately
   12 roses
120 ml (4 fl oz) water
Non-stick pan and a stove
Blender
Darning or embroidery
   needle
Waxed cotton cord

## METHOD:

1. Put the rose petals into the pan with the water and simmer over a low heat until softened.

2. Put the petals into the blender, add a splash of water if necessary and blend to a smooth, thick paste.

3. Pour back into the pan and simmer over a medium heat, stirring constantly until the water evaporates and the mixture has a clay-like consistency.

4. Once cooled, pinch off pieces of the mixture and roll into beads (they will shrink as they dry). Make one slightly larger bead to mark your start and end point.

**5.** Set the beads aside for 24–48 hours, until they feel firm, then push a needle through the centre of each one, making a hole wide enough to insert the cord.

**6.** Leave the beads on a sunny windowsill until completely dry.

**7.** When they are ready to be strung, tie off one end of your cord, leaving a 10-cm (4-in.) long tail.

**8.** Thread the beads onto the cord, tying a knot between each one.

**9.** After stringing the small beads, tie the cord ends to create a circle.

**10.** Thread both ends of the cord through the large bead and tie a knot to secure, trimming any excess.

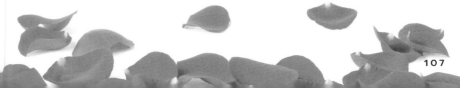

# BUILD A GARDEN LABYRINTH

A labyrinth is an ancient spiritual tool used by many faiths for contemplation, self-reflection, walking meditation and prayer. The imagery of the circle symbolizes wholeness, while the spiralling path represents a journey through life or a pilgrimage. Unlike a maze, which has multiple branches and dead ends to navigate, a labyrinth only has one route to the centre and back, so labyrinth walking engages the right hemisphere of the brain, which is believed to influence creativity, imagination, intuition and visualization. As well as enhancing peace of mind, self-awareness and mental well-being, there's evidence that labyrinth walking can help lower blood pressure, reduce anxiety and even decrease chronic pain. A labyrinth is also a beautiful garden feature that will encourage you to spend more time outside connecting with yourself and nature.

Labyrinths can be created using many different materials. Here are some ideas:

- **Mow the labyrinth design into a lawn or wildflower meadow.**
- **Sink bricks into the lawn or use paving slabs to create a labyrinth-design patio.**

- Plant quick-growing bamboo or hornbeam hedges, or fragrant, low-growing herbs like lavender, rosemary, thyme, or a dwarf variety of chamomile to edge and mark out the path.

- Use chalk, pebbles, pinecones or shells to mark out a labyrinth, then decorate it with pot plants or cut flowers.

Choose a design and use chalk, non-toxic spray paint or rope to mark out the pattern on the ground before you begin to mow, plant or install a pathway.

# Walking Meditation

Walking meditation is a beneficial practice for body and mind. As well as reducing stress and anxiety, it can help regulate blood pressure and improve cardiovascular health. Walking meditation also increases concentration, sharpens awareness and encourages mindfulness. So often we rush around, oblivious to our surroundings and the subtle details that mark the changing seasons. Allowing your mind to fully engage with your environment promotes a deeper connection with your garden and the natural world.

Walking meditation can be practised anywhere, from a community garden or allotment to a compact courtyard. Aim to walk for 10–20 minutes at least three times a week. Allow your gaze and body to relax as you take your first steps. Rather than focusing on your breath or a mantra, feel your surroundings and engage your senses. Notice the springy grass underfoot, plant stems tickling your legs or the velvet softness of rose petals brushing against your fingertips. Appreciate the heady fragrances of flowers and herbs, the whisper of the breeze blowing through ornamental grasses or the gentle hum of foraging bees and birds flitting from plant to plant. Observe dew drops glistening on a spider's web or the dancing reflections on the surface of a water feature. Enjoy the immediacy of these sights and sensations, acknowledging them and letting them go. If your thoughts drift, gently guide them back to the rhythm of the walk and your surroundings. Continue walking as long as you feel comfortable.

# BE A MINDFUL GARDENER

Gardening is a naturally meditative pastime but practising mindfulness while you garden can intensify the positive impact it has on both mental and emotional well-being. Mindfulness is a technique that encourages moment-by-moment awareness of your surroundings, helping you to be fully present, whether you're sowing, weeding, watering, pruning or harvesting. As you focus your attention on the task at hand, acknowledge your thoughts, feelings and the physical sensations you're experiencing. This will help to improve your mental clarity, enhance your objectivity and increase your awareness and acceptance of change, freeing you from negative thoughts. Follow these tips for more meaningful mindfulness:

- **Set aside distractions** – Switch off your phone, turn off your music and give the garden your full attention.

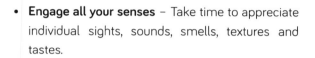

- **Engage all your senses** – Take time to appreciate individual sights, sounds, smells, textures and tastes.

- **Attune to nature** – Notice the natural rhythms of the sun and moon and the changing seasons.

- **Pay attention to the details** – Allow yourself to become immersed in your environment. Lie down in the grass and study the insects. Watch spring blossoms dance like confetti on the breeze. Notice a tiny flower blooming in a crack in the concrete. Concentrate on how it feels to plunge your hands into the soil.

- **Act with intention** – When you're ready to pick up your tools, set an intention to help you focus and remind yourself why you are carrying out the task – for example, to create a habitat for wildlife, grow food to nourish your body or pick a bunch of flowers to cheer up a friend.

# The Tomato Exercise

Mindfulness is about being present in every aspect of our daily activities. We can miss so much when we do things in haste and on autopilot. This exercise introduces mindful awareness, encouraging you to use all your senses when you're working in the garden or enjoying the produce you've grown. Increasing your capacity for mindfulness will help you to appreciate the garden's small delights, like the beauty and flavour explosion of a single sun-ripened tomato.

For this exercise, you'll need a cherry tomato (you could also use a berry, pea or broad bean).

- **Hold** – Place the tomato in the palm of your hand. Focus on it, imagining that you have never seen an object like it before.

- **Look** – Give it your full attention. Notice the shape, folds and ridges in the skin, subtle variations in colour, the highlights and shadows created when the light shines on it and any blemishes or unusual features.

- **Touch** – Roll it between your fingers, investigating the size, shape, and textures of the skin, calyx and stem.

- **Smell** – Bring it up to your nose and inhale the aroma. Notice any sensations in your mouth or stomach.

- **Taste** – Place it in your mouth. Explore it with your tongue, noticing its texture and the sensations in your mouth as you roll it around. Consciously take a bite. Notice the burst of flavour. As you begin to chew, appreciate the changes in texture and taste. Swallow, seeing how long the flavour remains in your mouth and how your body feels.

# FIND YOUR ZEN

Zen gardens originated in Japan as places for quiet contemplation. Their distinctive minimalistic style is designed to promote serenity and introspection. In stark contrast to most gardens, Zen gardens contain very few plants – perhaps just a clump of bamboo, a meticulously pruned bonsai tree or a pillowy mound of cushion moss. Instead, they are dominated by hard landscaping, comprised of sand, gravel, rock and wood, accented with bridges and lanterns. Raking patterns in sand or gravel to represent ripples in water and arranging rocks to symbolize mountains, trees and islands encourages mindfulness and is a wonderfully stress-relieving activity. If you'd like to create a Zen garden:

If you don't have sufficient outdoor space, why not create a tabletop Zen garden to keep on your desk and encourage you to take mindful breaks?

- **Keep it simple.** A key concept in Zen gardens is empty space as uncluttered spaces help to clear the mind. Choose a single statue or lantern to serve as a focal point for meditation.

- **Use contrasting colours and textures.** How about a scarlet-leaved Japanese acer tree juxtaposed against white gravel or a rough-hewn chunk of granite situated next to a carpet of velvety soft moss?

- **Conjure up a sense of mystery and magic.** This is achieved using a technique known as "hide and reveal" in which you create an illusion by partially concealing a garden feature so that it can only be seen from certain viewpoints.

# Get Down to Earth

Modern life physically disconnects humans from the Earth. We wear shoes, walk on pavements and live and work in multiple-storeyed buildings. Practising earthing, also known as grounding, can help you feel centred, balanced and more in touch with our planet's energy.

Earthing tips:

- Walk barefoot in the garden for at least 30 minutes.
- Stand with your feet flat. Curl, uncurl and wiggle your toes, paying attention to the sensations you feel as your skin makes contact with grass, soil, moss or stones.
- Stamp your feet on the ground and feel the Earth supporting you. Notice how your feet and legs feel.

# Garden Rituals

Rituals can give us a sense of control, help us to focus, deal with anxiety and increase our confidence. They can add meaning to our lives by turning everyday actions into something significant. Unlike habits, which are actions we do without thinking, rituals are mindful and symbolic.

Garden rituals can transform the mundane and help you appreciate and celebrate your garden, so why not:

- Snap a photo of your garden at the same time every day, week or month.

- Sow seeds to mark significant days or events.

- Pause for a moment of stillness to start and finish each gardening session.

# CULTIVATE A DEEPER CONNECTION WITH YOUR GARDEN

Introduced by Austrian philosopher Rudolf Steiner in 1924, biodynamics is an organic, holistic and spiritual approach to gardening, which places emphasis on tuning into the rhythms of nature and harnessing natural forces. Devotees believe that the principles and practices:

- **Respect the ecology of the environment.**

- **Encourage plants to develop natural resistance to pests and diseases rather than relying on pesticides and fungicides.**

- **Encourage people to form a deeper, more personal and mutually beneficial relationship with nature.**

- **Increase soil and plant health.**

- **Increase the yield, quality, nutrients and flavour of home-grown fruit and vegetables.**

- **Boost the fragrance of herbs and flowers.**

# BIODYNAMICS FOR BEGINNERS

- **Moon sowing** – Sow seeds two to three days before the full moon.
- **Compost** – Compost garden waste to put back what you have taken out of the soil.
- **Crop rotation** – Plant crops in groups such as leaves, roots, seeds and fruits or flowers. Each group depletes specific nutrients so rotate yearly to allow soil to recover its fertility.
- **Natural fertilizer** – Fill a bucket with crushed nettle and comfrey leaves. Cover with water and weigh down with a brick. Brew for a month, then dilute one part liquid to 10 parts water. Vigorously stir before applying liberally to your plants.
- **Companion planting** – Plant herbs and flowers which lure pests away from your crops or encourage natural predators like hoverflies and ladybirds.

Keen to learn more? Contact your local biodynamic association.

# FEEL-GOOD FACT

Bees and butterflies hold spiritual significance in many cultures and often appear in religious texts. Bees represent dedication, resilience, blessings of fertility, and prosperity. Butterflies represent renewal and new beginnings, and their lifecycle serves as a metaphor for human spiritual transformation, reminding us that nothing is permanent and just as a caterpillar must go through a dark and difficult phase before emerging as a butterfly, so too must we face challenges and tribulations in order to reach our full potential. Since ancient times, both bees and butterflies have been viewed as spirit guides and winged messengers between our world and the otherworld.

# Spiritually Uplifting Insects

Butterflies are beloved garden visitors. Seeing one of these ethereal creatures dance from flower to flower inspires a sense of joy, hope and positivity, particularly if you've been facing challenges or feeling down. Bees should also be welcomed, as they play a vital role in our health and well-being. As important pollinators, their presence is key to plant growth, reproduction and the production of flowers, fruits and vegetables, which provide us with food, clothes, building materials and medicines. The world's insects are declining at an alarming rate, with many species facing extinction due to climate change, habitat loss, toxic pesticides and disease but our gardens can act as important bridges between nature reserves and wild habitats.

# CREATE AN INSECT HAVEN

If you're keen to attract bees and butterflies to your garden, planting an abundance of flowers is wise but some are more beneficial than others. Showy double or triple blooms are of little use to our insect friends, who struggle to access the nectar and pollen. Choose elegant single-flowered varieties such as:

- Bee balm (*Monarda didyma*)
- Borage (*Borago officinalis*)
- Butterfly bush (*Buddleja davidii*)
- Catmint (*Nepeta spp.*)
- Chives (*Allium schoenoprasum*)
- Common ivy (*Hedera helix*)
- Cosmos (*Cosmos spp.*)
- Honeywort (*Cerinthe major*)
- Ice plant (*Hylotelephium spectabile*)
- Lavender (*Lavandula angustifolia*)
- Red bistort (*Persicaria amplexicaulis*)
- Sunflower (*Helianthus annuus*)
- Verbena bonariensis (*Verbena bonariensis*)

Provide a selection of plants that flower throughout the seasons and plant them in blocks, so bees and butterflies don't have too far to fly between flowers. Insects enjoy warmth, so choose a sunny, sheltered spot. Never use insecticides; if you have an infestation of aphids, encourage natural predators like ladybirds or plant calendula or nasturtiums as sacrificial plants.

Bees and butterflies need fresh water, so create a drinking station by filling a shallow saucer with rainwater and pebbles. You may also like to buy or make a bee nesting box and butterfly hibernation house.

# Part Five: Get Social While You Garden

Gardening is often considered a solitary activity but there are endless opportunities to form bonds with fellow enthusiasts. You could work collaboratively, helping others by getting involved with community or therapeutic gardening projects. One of the greatest joys of gardening is the chance to share your passion, celebrating triumphs and commiserating over failures. Humans are inherently social so making connections with like-minded individuals is vital for our well-being. Studies suggest that people who have an active social life and form meaningful relationships with others live longer, healthier lives. Having a strong support system can regulate our emotions, boost self-esteem, help us overcome challenges, reduce anxiety and depression, lower stress levels and even strengthen the immune system. Gardening is a powerful uniter, bringing people from different backgrounds together and granting them common ground. It also links us to our ancestors and leaves a green legacy for future generations.

# Find Your Tribe

If you're searching for a sense of belonging and social connectedness, look no further than the gardening community. Here are some ways to meet fellow gardeners:

- Join a local gardening club or horticultural society.

- Attend a flower show, horticultural festival, exhibition or lecture.

- Become a member of a horticultural charity.

- Sign up to a class or workshop.

- Explore online gardening communities.

- Participate in a community gardening project.

- Care for a conservation area.

- Take on an allotment.

- Volunteer – From running a school gardening club to helping at a local park, there are no shortage of volunteering opportunities.

# Growing Happier and Healthier Together

According to studies, the health risks of loneliness and prolonged social isolation are comparable to those of smoking, obesity and physical inactivity, reducing quality of life and decreasing life expectancy. Spending time with others is vital to protecting physical and mental health. Allotments and community gardens provide an opportunity to interact with like-minded people in a social setting. Simply exchanging a smile and friendly greeting with your allotment neighbours or fellow gardening group volunteers can boost your mood and stimulate the emotional centre of the brain to release neurotransmitters which encourage a more positive outlook and real feelings of happiness.

# Teamwork Makes the Dream Work!

Working on a group project will give you a sense of purpose, increase your self-confidence, improve your social and horticultural skills and bring fun and fulfilment to your life. Perhaps you're keen to improve your local environment for the benefit of people and wildlife by transforming an area of wasteland into a wildflower meadow? Tending a community vegetable garden or restoring the grounds of a historic building might be your sort of thing. Or maybe you'd like to help people recovering from ill health by volunteering for a therapeutic horticulture programme. With teamwork, anything is possible.

# FEEL-GOOD FACT

Visionary nineteenth-century nurse, Florence Nightingale, recognized the healing power of the natural world when she said, "Nature alone cures." Today, healthcare professionals prescribe gardening for their patients and horticultural therapy has become a recognized practice, widely used to support people with physical and mental health problems and learning disabilities.

# Give Back Through Gardening

Gardening is a fantastic way to give back to your community and make a positive impact on the lives of others. You can make your experience of gardening more meaningful by:

- Donating surplus garden or allotment produce to a food bank or community food pantry or sharing it with family, friends and neighbours.

- Helping an elderly, ill or disabled person maintain their garden.

- Fundraising for charity by opening your garden and charging visitors an entry fee.

- Creating a community garden or adopting an area of waste ground.

- Sharing your knowledge and skills by teaching gardening to children or adults.

# EXPAND YOUR GARDEN HORIZONS

Why not use your love of gardening as inspiration for your next holiday? Bond with new friends as you visit breathtaking gardens and learn how their design embodies local culture and history. Plan your own itinerary or book an expert-led guided tour.

Here are 12 must-see gardens to inspire your future travels:

- Royal Botanical Gardens at Kew – London, UK
- The New York Botanical Garden – New York City, USA
- Chateau de Versailles – Versailles, France
- Dubai Miracle Garden – Dubai, UAE
- The Singapore Botanic Gardens – Singapore
- Kenroku-en Garden – Kanazawa, Japan
- Claude Monet's Garden – Giverny, France
- Kirstenbosch National Botanical Garden – Cape Town, South Africa
- The Eden Project – Cornwall, UK
- Keukenhof Gardens – Lisse, Netherlands
- Jardin Majorelle – Marrakech, Morocco
- Australian National Botanical Gardens – Canberra, Australia

# Branch Out Online

The internet can take you on a virtual voyage of horticultural discovery. There are millions of gardening websites to browse, podcasts to hear and green-fingered bloggers, Instagrammers and YouTubers to follow. Platforms such as Heygo make it possible to join live-streamed tours of some of the world's most spectacular botanical gardens and parks. Social media groups are a popular way to connect with gardeners around the world, whether you're looking for advice on houseplant care, design inspiration for an urban balcony garden or want to get involved in a tomato breeding project. Before joining a group, be sure to read their guidelines to check that they are the right community for you.

Social media hashtags make it easy to find or share specific information within the online gardening community. Use or look out for:

#gardenlife          #plantsmakepeoplehappy

#instagardeners      #houseplantcommunity

#planttherapy        #flowerphotography

#plantshelfie        #plantsofinstagram

#growwhatyoueat      #gardeninggoals

Keep a note of your must-follow
garden influencers here:

..............................................................................
..............................................................................
..............................................................................
..............................................................................
..............................................................................
..............................................................................
..............................................................................
..............................................................................
..............................................................................
..............................................................................
..............................................................................
..............................................................................
..............................................................................
..............................................................................
..............................................................................
..............................................................................
..............................................................................
..............................................................................
..............................................................................
..............................................................................
..............................................................................

# BE THE CHANGE

As a gardener, you can play a role in improving your local area and making a tangible impact on the wider world. Community gardens provide beauty and sustenance, help to regenerate run-down areas, prevent anti-social behaviour and improve the local economy. Private gardens attract wildlife and help create more climate-resilient urban areas by preventing flooding and reducing heat. However, it's important to acknowledge the potential negative eco-impact of gardening and keep your horticultural hobby as sustainable as possible. Here are some eco-friendly gardening tips:

- **Switch to peat-free compost** – Peat plays a vital role in the fight against the climate crisis so choose peat-free compost or make your own by composting kitchen scraps and garden waste.

- **Save water** – Install water butts to collect rainwater and water non-edible plants with "grey water" from baths, showers and sinks.

- **Buy local** – Many plants are brought in from abroad, creating a significant carbon footprint. Where possible, choose locally grown plants or exchange cuttings with friends.

- **Avoid plastic** – Plastic pots break easily and often end up in landfill. Look for sustainable packaging such as biodegradable coir pots. Sow seeds in wooden trays, paper pots or repurposed household waste such as egg cartons and toilet roll tubes.

- **Choose your tools wisely** – Overconsumption is a leading cause of overflowing landfill. Buy second hand or borrow from a fellow gardener or tool library. Where practical, use manual rather than electrical tools and keep them well-maintained to prolong their life.

# BECOME A CITIZEN SCIENTIST

Citizen science gives the public an opportunity to voluntarily participate in scientific research by collecting and analyzing valuable data. Participating in a citizen science project can help you to feel more connected to other gardeners and increase your knowledge of the natural environment. As well as highlighting the ways in which you can improve your own garden, data collected may have far-reaching effects, helping scientists to determine the ways in which we can all garden in a more sustainable way, better support wildlife, or grow more flavourful, nutritious and disease-resistant fruit and vegetables. As individuals, we often feel powerless to tackle the most critical challenges of our time, such as climate change, water scarcity, hunger crisis, biodiversity loss and species extinction. Citizen science projects allow

gardeners worldwide to work together, combining collective action with scientific research to make a meaningful impact both locally and globally.

Which aspects of gardening are you most passionate about? Whether you're keen to record weather data or wildlife sightings, monitor soil conditions, observe plant life cycles or take part in seed-growing trials, there's a citizen science project for you. Online search engines or citizen science project databases are the best place to find information about projects that are actively recruiting volunteers. You can use keywords or filters to narrow down your search to specific topics of interest but don't be afraid to expand your geographic scope as opportunities may be local, national or international.

# Swap Shop

As the song says, the best things in life are free!
Yet many gardeners spend a fortune buying seeds
and plants each year. Seed and plant swaps are
a fantastic way to acquire new varieties for free,
share your excess seeds and cuttings and build
relationships with other local gardeners. Commercial
seed packets often contain more seed than you need
for your own use and the germination rate is likely to
fall in subsequent years, so it makes sense to trade
or give away any leftover seed. It's also a perfect
opportunity to exchange knowledge and tips.

# FEEL-GOOD FACT

Did you know that seed saving and swapping isn't just
a cost-effective way to propagate edible and ornamental
plants for your garden? It also plays a vital role in the
conservation of precious heirloom varieties. Heirloom seeds
are a living link to our history, telling the stories of people,
places and important events. In many parts of the world,
our plant heritage is under threat as industrial agriculture
and seed marketing regulations threaten the existence
of these genetically diverse, open-pollinated garden seed
varieties. By saving and sharing seeds, you're helping to
improve the biodiversity of our planet.

# A SIMPLE GUIDE TO SAVING SEEDS

- Plan your seed saving at the beginning of the growing season. Think about the crops you'd like to grow for their seeds and where you'll plant them.

- Only save the seeds of open-pollinated varieties of fruits, vegetables and flowers as F1 (hybrid) varieties won't grow true to type. For beginners, some of the easiest seeds to save are tomato, chilli, pea and bean or flowers such as calendula, cosmos, nigella, snapdragon, poppy and sunflower.

- Save seeds from the healthiest, most vigorous plants. It's important to choose a mature flower, fruit or vegetable as, if you harvest seeds when they are still immature, they won't germinate.

- Collect ripe seeds on a dry day. Lay seedheads or pods out to dry in the greenhouse, on a sunny windowsill or in the airing cupboard, then gently crush to release the seeds. Gather seeds from fleshy fruits and vegetables by scooping them into a sieve and rinsing away the pulp, then leave them to dry on paper towels.

- Once the seeds are completely dry, clean off any bits of husk, stem or leaf, as this material can harbour moulds and cause rot. Discard any seeds that show signs of insect damage.

- Place the seeds in a clean, dry, paper envelope, label with the variety and date collected, then store inside an airtight container with a packet of silica gel to absorb any excess moisture. Keep the seeds in a cool, dry place until you are ready to sow or share them. The fresher they are, the better the germination rate is likely to be.

# ORIGAMI SEED ENVELOPES

Nothing holds more promise than a packet of seeds. They make wonderful gifts and are easy to slip inside a greeting card or through a friend or neighbour's letterbox.

## YOU'LL NEED:

Sheets of paper – Get creative by using pages ripped out of old gardening magazines, seed catalogues and books or make the envelopes extra special by decorating plain paper with drawings, personal messages and growing instructions.

## METHOD:

1. Cut your sheet of paper into a square.

2. Fold the paper in half diagonally, making a triangle. Position the triangle with the longest side facing you.

3. Fold the bottom left corner of the triangle across to meet the centre of the opposite side, so that the top edge of the fold is parallel with the bottom of the triangle.

4. Repeat with the right corner, folding it across the first fold, so the edges line up.

5. Fold down the front envelope flap and tuck it into the triangular pocket you have created by making the previous fold.

6. Open the envelope and fill it with seeds.

7. To close the envelope, fold down the remaining flap and tuck it into the same triangular pocket as the first flap.

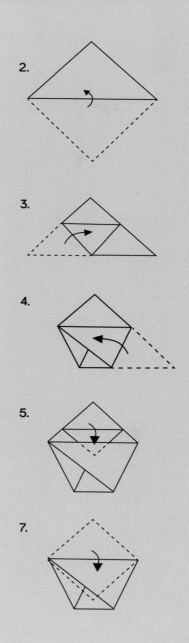

# Sharing is Caring

No matter the size of your garden or what you grow, at some point you're bound to find yourself with an abundance of produce. While it's fun to share or swap your garden bounty with friends and neighbours (perhaps you have a glut of courgettes, while they're overrun with beans!), why not transform some of your excess into creative homemade gifts. Everyone loves delicious homemade jams, jellies, chutneys and pickles but fruits and herbs can also be used to make flavourful infused oils, vinegars or alcohol. If you have a proliferation of vibrant flowers, brighten someone's day with a hand-tied bouquet or press them to make unique greetings cards or gifts. You could also pot up offshoots from admired houseplants.

# PRESS FLOWERS FROM YOUR GARDEN

Pressing flowers is a wonderful way to capture their beauty. Use them to make pressed flower pictures or to decorate greetings cards and bookmarks.

1. Choose unblemished flowers coming into full bloom. Pick them in the morning as soon as the dew has dried.

2. Open a large, heavy book at a middle page. Place a sheet of parchment paper down, then arrange the flowers on top, making sure they aren't overlapping. Top with another sheet of parchment paper and close the book, weighing it down with something heavy.

3. The flowers will be ready to use within three weeks.

# SUMMER BERRY JAM

Turning your homegrown fruit into jewel-coloured jam is the best way to preserve the summer, bottling a little shot of sunshine to enjoy during long winter months. It's also perfect served with freshly baked scones or used to fill a sponge cake.

## YOU'LL NEED:

1 kg (2 lb) mixed
    berries (blackberries,
    strawberries, blueberries,
    raspberries, blackcurrants,
    redcurrants, cranberries)
    Juice of 1 lemon
1 kg (2 lb) jam sugar

The jam will keep for a year unopened. Once opened, store in the fridge and use within one month.

## METHOD:

1. Sterilize four jam jars and lids by putting them through a hot dishwasher cycle, or by washing in hot soapy water, rinsing, then putting them in the oven at a low temperature until dry.

2. Wash and drain the berries and tip them into a large pan. Add the lemon juice and sugar, then simmer over a medium heat, stirring occasionally, until the fruit juices start to flow and the sugar has melted.

3. Turn up the heat and bring to a boil. Boil for 15–20 minutes, until the jam reaches setting point. Test for this by putting a teaspoon of the mixture onto a chilled saucer. Once it's cooled a little, push your finger through it. If it wrinkles, it's ready. If not, return to the heat, boil for 5 minutes more, then test again.

4. Pour the jam into the sterilized jam jars and seal while still hot.

5. Label the jars and decorate them with fabric lid covers secured with twine.

# CREATE A CUT FLOWER PATCH

The gift of a beautiful, fragrant bunch of flowers will bring a smile to anyone's face but shop-bought bunches are expensive and often unsustainable. Growing your own blooms is environmentally friendly and costs a fraction of the price.

You could dot flowers for cutting throughout your garden but it's much easier to maintain a dedicated patch and you won't risk your borders looking bald when you start picking! It also means that you can grow blooms in a wide range of colours without worrying about them clashing with the rest of the plants in your garden. Practically all flowers prefer to grow in full or at least partial sun so take care to position your patch away from shady areas and sow the tallest species at the back of the bed and the shortest at the front. Shelter is also important, as strong wind can snap stems and damage petals, and be sure to use an organic slug and snail deterrent to prevent your seedlings being munched. Regular watering, mulching with organic compost and deadheading will keep plants healthy and prolong flowering.

**Top choices for stunning bouquets:**

**Bulbs** – Tulips, daffodils, scented narcissi, hyacinths, snowdrops, ranunculus, gladioli

**Annuals** – Cosmos, ammi majus, sweet peas, cornflowers, nigella, calendulas, sunflowers, snapdragons, honeywort, zinnias, nicotiana, violas

**Perennials** – Dahlias, roses, peonies, echinacea, delphiniums, penstemons, salvias, verbena bonariensis, echinops

**Foliage** – Bells of Ireland, lady's mantle, euphorbia, rosemary, fennel, viburnum, eucalyptus, dusty miller

# CREATE A HAND-TIED BOUQUET

Flower arranging doesn't need to be intimidating. Designing an exquisite arrangement is easier than you think and the principles are the same whether you're creating a flamboyant bouquet of mixed flowers and foliage or a delicate posy of snowdrops, sweet peas or violas.

- **Pick** – Cut your flowers in the early morning or evening, when the air is cool, and their stems are full of water. Strip off the lower leaves and put the flowers straight into a bucket of water so they don't start to dry out.

- **Condition** – Conditioning flowers extends their vase life. First, sear the stems by dipping the bottom 10 per cent into boiling water for between 5–30 seconds (the tougher, woodier and thicker the stem, the longer it needs), which will increase water absorption and keep the blooms looking fresher for longer. Then immediately plunge into cold water and leave to rest.

- **Arrange** – For a voluminous bouquet, arrange the flowers in a spiral. Choose three blooms as the central focal point, then start adding additional stems at a 45-degree angle, rotating the bunch as you go. Once you're happy with your arrangement, secure with twine and trim the stems to the same length.

- **Transport** – To ensure the flowers reach the recipient looking as fresh as they did when you picked them, transport the bouquet in a vase or jam jar of water. Adding a splash of white vinegar will prevent bacteria growth, which can turn stems slimy and make the water smell.

# Celebrating and Commemorating With Plants

Plants have long been used as a meaningful way to mark significant life events. From milestone birthdays, weddings and anniversaries to retirement or moving house, there are named varieties available to commemorate any occasion. Planting a tree is a symbolic way to celebrate the birth of a baby as it will grow and mature alongside them. Trees and shrubs also make beautiful living memorials for lost loved ones, providing a physical place to gather, remember and reflect on their life. A container, border, or even a whole garden can be planted as a lasting tribute to a beloved family member, friend or companion animal.

# SAY IT WITH FLOWERS

Floriography, also known as the language of flowers, is the art of communicating emotions through the symbolism of plants and trees. Nearly every sentiment can be expressed with flowers and using plant choice to convey your feelings will make a gift or memorial even more thoughtful. Some popular species to consider are:

- **Rose** – love, gratitude, compassion, joy, friendship and appreciation
- **Forget-me-not** – respect, faithfulness remembrance and eternal love
- **Clematis** – intelligence, ingenuity and wisdom
- **Orchid** – thoughtfulness, prosperity and everlasting love
- **Camellia** – love, devotion, admiration and care
- **Birch** – gentleness, new beginnings, rebirth and growth
- **Rowan** – courage, wisdom and protection
- **Apple** – knowledge, good health and future happiness

# CONCLUSION

We can learn much from our gardens, from the joys of growing flowers, plants and produce to nurture our minds, bodies and souls to the importance of community and the positive social and environmental changes we can achieve when we connect with other horticultural enthusiasts.

As you now know, the benefits of plants don't need to stop outdoors. You can bring nature inside your home or workplace by growing houseplants, tending topiary trees or sprouting herbs and micro greens on your kitchen windowsill.

Hopefully, this book has encouraged you to look at gardening in a new light and begin your own journey of personal development, whether that be creating a restorative garden haven to escape the stresses of everyday life, gaining clarity through

mindfulness, nourishing and nurturing your body, expanding and sharing your knowledge or simply spending time surrounded by nature to remind yourself of the infinite beauty in our world. As you learn and grow, you will become more resilient and grateful, and with that resilience and gratitude comes a happier life. Whether planting trees, growing flowers, setting up a community kitchen garden or volunteering for a therapeutic horticulture programme, you will also be putting down roots and creating a legacy that will benefit you, your community, wildlife and future generations. Above all, enjoy reaping the rewards of this life-enhancing pastime and remember that a garden is a powerful metaphor for your own life – consistent (self-)care is vital to ensure that you will thrive and flourish.

**Grow well...**

## GARDENING FOR MIND, BODY AND SOUL: HOW TO NURTURE YOUR WELL-BEING WITH NATURE

ISBN: 978-1-80007-162-9
Hardback

We have long been aware of the positive effects of spending time in nature and how it can be a powerful antidote to the stresses of modern life. Science now tells us that cultivating a green space of our own can be restorative and even transformative for our physical and mental well-being, with a proven ability to reduce depression and anxiety, boost our happiness levels and provide a feeling of balance and calm.

## BRING THE WILD INTO YOUR GARDEN: SIMPLE TIPS FOR CREATING A WILDLIFE HAVEN

ISBN: 978-1-78783-667-9
Hardback

Whether you long to see butterflies flit across your flowerbeds or hear birdsong all year round, there's something endlessly rewarding about playing host to wildlife. With practical projects and helpful tips for gardens big and small, this guide will help boost local biodiversity and benefit countless native species.

# IMAGE CREDITS

Have you enjoyed this book?
If so, why not write a review on your favourite website?

If you're interested in finding out more about our books,
find us on Facebook at **Summersdale Publishers**, on
Twitter at **@Summersdale** and on Instagram and TikTok
at **@summersdalebooks** and get in touch. We'd love to
hear from you!

Thanks very much for buying this Summersdale book.
**www.summersdale.com**